How to Write a Book

A Blueprint For How To Write, Publish And Market Your Own Non-fiction Book

Jonathan Reid

Respective authors own all copyrights not held by the publisher.

The information herein is offered for informational purposes solely, and is universal as so. The presentation of the information is without contract or any type of guarantee assurance.

The trademarks that are used are without any consent, and the publication of the trademark is without permission or backing by the trademark owner. All trademarks and brands within this book are for clarifying purposes only and are the owned by the owners themselves, not affiliated with this document.

CONTENTS

INTRODUCTION

These days, many people are seeking to write books. They have been noted to be wonderful sources of residual income, they can assist you with positioning yourself as an expert in your field, and they can help you tell your story. There are many reasons as to why you may want to write a book, too. You may be looking to add value to the products and services you offer your clients or to diversify your portfolio. Regardless of what your reasoning is, one thing remains the same. That is, the way the book needs to be written!

How to Write a Book: How To Write, Publish And Market Your Very Own Non-fiction Book is exactly that. A blueprint to guide you through the entire process of designing your work of art and then selling it to the masses. You will be walked through every step of the process to ensure that you create a high quality book that will have people excited to purchase it.

Writing a book is a powerful way to position yourself in your field and to add an additional income stream to your life. When you write a book, you add value to people's lives by enriching them with information they may not have had access to previously. It allows people to get to know you in a sense, while also giving you the opportunity to get to know your people.

As you are reading through this book, take your time. It is highly suggested that you read through this book once to get an idea of what you will need to do, then start from the beginning and follow it as a guide. The second time through, stop after each chapter and section and do some work towards your own book. That way, you can ensure that each step of the process is accurate and that your book will be high quality for anyone who reads it.

Lastly, please be sure to enjoy this book! The process of writing a book is intended to be joyful. You should not feel as though you are burdened to write something. Instead, take it lightly and have fun with it! Allow it to be a joyous process and you will gain more than you may have ever expected from writing your book.

here.

CHAPTER ONE: THE REVOLUTION OF BOOK PUBLISHING

The technology around book publishing has changed dramatically over several years. In fact, the evolution in the past three decades alone has been astonishing. There are so many different parts of the process that have evolved that it is truly a different art than it was just three decades ago. Let's take a moment to look back through the history of publishing books since the 1980s.

Book Publishing in the 1980s

In the 1980s, books were always on paper. There were no screens for books to be read on, therefore there was no one reading digital books. Digital books weren't even a thing then. Indie book stores and retail chain book stores were where everyone went when they wanted to purchase a book. The library was extremely popular as well. Purchasing books was costly and storing them took up a great deal of space. Using the library allowed people to borrow books and return them. While libraries still exist today, they certainly aren't nearly as popular as they once were.

Books in the 1980s needed to be published by massive publishing chains. Without the backing of a publishing chain, a book would never be seen by the general public. Publishing chains were not only responsible for helping individuals turn their manuscripts into paperback and hard covered novels, but they were responsible for many other things as well. Publishing chains would put their "seal of approval" on a book and then sell it in massive retail chain stores, as well as popular independent stores. Publishing chains had departments specifically responsible for establishing relationships with these book stores and allowing them to sell their books on the shelves of these popular stores.

Without a publishing chain, an author would never be discovered and their books would never be sold. It would be nearly impossible for the author to get their book printed into book format, never mind gain a spot on the shelves of massive retail stores and popular indie stores that were selling thousands of copies of books per year.

At this point, books were often purchased from department stores. As a result, these department stores would have wealthy book sections filled with best sellers and the most popular titles of that month. If you wanted to have your book discovered and purchased, you needed to compete with the thousands of others on the shelves.

If your book was not competitive enough, publishing houses wouldn't even consider your work. Their money came from selling books, therefore they only wanted books that were best-seller quality. If they saw true potential in you, you might be able to work together with a publishing chain. Because of this, many authors would send their manuscript to dozens of publishing chains in hopes of one or two liking their work. If none liked their work, they would have to start over again or send it to more chains until someone decided they liked it. Many authors would send their books to as many as 18 chains before someone decided they liked what the author was writing about and would publish the book.

All in all, the book publishing industry was extremely fierce in the 1980s. If you didn't show extreme promise in the eyes of the top publishing chains in the industry, you likely wouldn't produce a book. If you did, the book may not be as popular as it would be if you were able to get a contract with one of the top-notch publishing chains.

Book Publishing in the 1990s

Through the 1990s, chain bookstores were rapidly growing as well. Their atmospheres were library-like, only you purchased books as opposed to borrowing them. These bookstores had thousands of titles that could be purchased at any given time. They were almost always known to carry the best sellers and all of the most popular literature of all time. If you were looking for a book, this is the type of store you would likely visit in order to find said book.

Because of the rising popularity of bookstore chains like this, it became common for the larger chains to heavily discount their titles. As a result, the entire industry had to start charging less and less in order to remain competitive. This meant that there was a greater competition to have best-selling titles because they guaranteed high-volume sales and therefore higher profits. This also meant that many smaller independent businesses were being run out of business because they could no longer afford to maintain their overhead fees due to the lower profits they were earning from their sales.

In the 1990s, the publishing industry was starting to change. While it was still highly important for individuals to work together with a publishing chain, the way that books were being sold was evolving. With the rise of the internet and Amazon.com, books were starting to be sold online. As a result, many publishing chains were beginning to establish deals with online companies so that books could be sold there as well. This made purchasing books a great deal easier, and it pushed people's audiences a lot further.

Although the printed books continued to flourish at this time, the industry could tell that the internet was playing a major role in the total evolution of the book publishing industry. People were starting to suspect that CD-ROMs, online books, and other electronic books (e-books) would come to the surface and rise in popularity. At this time, people were still purchasing thousands of printed books per year, but the market was definitely starting to head in a new direction.

Book Publishing in the 2000s

By the early 2000s, book publishing was changing entirely. Electronic publishing was widely used and rapidly growing in popularity. Even text books for educational programs were being created online.

Print-on-demand became a popular method of printing which meant that publishers and suppliers would only print the books that were ordered. This saved publishing houses and printers thousands of dollars as they were not printing copious numbers of titles in hopes that all the copies would sell. Print-on-demand also had an added benefit of increasing the amount of time a book would remain for sale. In the past, books would be deemed "out of print" whenever sales would start to dwindle because the publishing house did not want to waste money printing books that were not selling as well. With print-on-demand however, they would simply print the necessary amount of stock and this would stop them from having to play the guessing game, as well as keep them from spending unnecessary money.

During the 2000s, e-book technologies evolved and e-readers were introduced. Amazon.com, one of the first and largest online book-selling platforms established what they call Kindle readers. These came along with the introduction of the Kindle section on their website which hosts the sales of hundreds of thousands of book titles.

In addition to the evolved formats in which books were being created and sold, publishing chains were evolving as well. In 2001, several publishing chains that were in direct competition agreed to bypass all the established online booksellers and start selling their products directly on Yahoo! website.

The face of the entire industry changed with the introduction of the internet. The importance of a publishing chain was no longer as relevant when you were seeking to print a book. While it was still beneficial to have a publishing chain behind you to gain their publicity and expertise, it was no longer necessary in order for books to be published. At this time, publishing chains were still popular but it was clear that they were starting to fade into the background of the entire industry.

Book Publishing Now

Now we are in the 2010s and the entire world of publishing is enormously different. Unlike the 1980s where you would never sell a single book if you didn't have a publishing chain behind you, nowadays anyone can sell a book. This means that the face of the industry is entirely different.

At one time, publishing chains determined who would or wouldn't get published. You only had to compete against the ones who were accepted by publishing houses, as anyone who wasn't accepted simply didn't have a book for sale. Nowadays, you have to compete against hundreds of thousands of self-published authors, as well as indie publishers and the publishing chains that are still out there. Publishing chains continue to sell thousands of copies of their best-sellers every year as they are still effective at endorsing books and marketing them on a large scale. However, many self-published authors are seeing a great return on their own publications as well.

There are many platforms on which you can write and publish a book now. Amazon.com and Barnesandnoble.com used to be the most popular, but nowadays there are several other indie publishing websites that will host your book and allow it for sale. Audio books have also risen in popularity. While they were initially released in the late 1990s and early 2000s, they have now become extremely popular. Listeners love having the option to purchase the audio book and listen to it while they are doing other things such as working out or driving to work.

The way we write, publish, market, and consume books is entirely different from how it was back in the 1980s. Even though that was just three decades ago, the entire face of the industry has completely changed. While these changes may present new and unique challenges, they also bring about an incredible opportunity for individuals to write books that can now be sold on virtually any platform.

CHAPTER TWO: MODERN BOOK PUBLISHING

As you are well aware, the revolution of book publishing completely changed the face of the publishing industry. Once the industry was able to establish itself in the online space, everything evolved so that the process of publishing was significantly easier and virtually anyone could do it. To get an idea of what that means for you, let's explore the world of modern book publishing.

The Writing Process

In the past, the writing process was significantly messier. Hundreds of pages would be typed out or hand written for the manuscript. If a mistake was made, it would either be crossed out and fixed or the entire page would be scrapped and the writer would have to completely start over again. The pages would have to be clipped into a binder or otherwise kept together and then mailed through the rest of the publishing steps. Getting the manuscript to the next stage was costly and it took a significant amount of time. If you had to do any research to write your book, you would have to purchase or borrow books in order to discover the information you needed. Overall, the process would take a year or longer for a simple novel. Any of the larger novels would be written over a span of several years.

Now, the writing process is extremely simple. You hop onto your computer and fire up a program like Microsoft Word or Pages and you start writing. If you make a mistake, you backspace to erase it and then fix the mistake. You can rewrite entire parts of the page without having to scrap the page and start all over again, further lengthening the process. If any research needs to be done you can simply key your specific needs into a search engine and all of your answers pop up immediately. You can research several hundreds of data platforms in a short time period. When you are ready to send it out to the next stages in the process, you can simply put the document into an e-mail and send it off. The entire process is a lot simpler and significantly easier. People are writing short novels in as little as a few weeks to a month, and longer novels in just a few months' time. While there are still writers who take a significant amount of time to release books, many are pumping out books quickly.

In addition to the writing process being simple, there is actually an entirely new opportunity in the publishing world. Now, you can hire "ghostwriters" to write your entire book for you! Essentially, you provide them with the information you would like to have included in your book, they write the book, and you push it through the rest of the process. When a book is written this way, you carry a contract that gives you full rights to the book and all of the content inside of the book. The ghostwriter relinquishes the book so that they can no longer claim the rights to it. You are able to take full credit for the book.

Editing and Formatting

At one time, you would have to send your book to an editor who would edit your book and then it might get sent back for you to re-write it. They may also include notes about how the book should be formatted. In general, the formatting was quite easy because you were only selling print copies if you were selling anything at all.

Editing these days is quite simple. In most cases, authors can simply run their document through a program like Grammarly and the bulk of the editing process is done. If you want to go further, you can e-mail it to an editor and have them go through it for you.

Generally, that editor will do the rewriting process due to the ease of it all now. They no longer have to retype hundreds of pages after making notes on them. Instead, they simply erase errors and replace them with proper grammar and spelling. They can then send it back to you for a final read.

Formatting is much different in modern times, as well. In the past, formatting was done when you were printing. You would simply not print any more on a certain page and that was that. Nowadays, you must insert page breaks, clickable table of contents, and other elements to complete books. The introduction of e-books and electronic consumption meant that books needed to be formatted in a certain way that would allow them to maintain the appearance of a proper and completed book. While the process of formatting is not difficult by any means, it does take more effort than it did in the past.

Publishing

As you read in the last chapter, publishing in the past was a major ordeal. You had to work to get a deal with a publisher, and then they had a significant amount of work to do. They would print copies of your book, get it into bookstores, and make sure that the marketing process was well looked after. Aside from writing the book and getting a deal with a publishing chain, there really wasn't a lot of work left for the writer.

Nowadays, it completely depends. Publishing chains still exist and if you choose to go through one you will still have to go through most of the same processes as you did in the past. Most of the chains and boutique publishing houses still prefer that a physical copy of the manuscript be sent to them, so you will have to print it and send it in just like you would have to in the past.

Where publishing is completely different is when it comes to publishing a book yourself. Unlike in the past where this was unheard of, this is now an extremely popular option. There are many ways that self-publishing works, it largely depends on what platform you choose to use. It also depends on what formats you want your book to be available in. If you want to publish a print book, you will need to work together with a self-publishing company that will allow you to print books. Createspace is a highly popular option that allows writers to purchase print copies of their books. If you want to have e-books and audiobooks, you can also use Createspace. However, the more popular option is to use Amazon Kindle. Amazon provides excellent publishing opportunities for people to publish everything they are looking for. Many even choose to purchase print copies from Createspace and then sell those through Amazon Kindle.

Aside from Createspace and Amazon, there are many other self-publishing companies out there. Ultimately, these companies assist you with making your book accessible to the public. When you work with these companies, they have extremely simple programs that guide you through the process of making your book available for sale. Then, all you have to do is market your book.

Something worth noting is that it can be a benefit to use multiple publishing companies. While the aforementioned two appear to be the largest, they are not the only options. Publishing through multiple companies allows you to make the book more readily available to more people. Additionally, publishing in at least two of the three consumable formats allows you to have a higher reach. The most popular choices these days appears to be e-book and audiobook. Most people these days are either into reading on the go or listening to their books so they don't have to read at all. Making your book available in both formats will increase your ability to sell copies.

Marketing

At one time, the author had virtually nothing to do with the marketing process. Aside from partaking in book signings and letting their family and friends know, the entire process was taken care of by the publishing chain. The publishing chain would tell authors what to do and where to be and the author would then do it.

The author themselves needed virtually no knowledge in the marketing scene because they were not in charge of the marketing aspect of their book at all.

This is completely different now. With self-publishing, you are the only one responsible for marketing your book. While you can hire a marketing team, this isn't always a cost-effective plan for people. Instead, you will want to learn how to effectively market your own book. Later in this book, you are going to learn exactly how you can market your own book after you have written and published it.

Marketing is important. Books that are published and not marketed are ones that will fade into the background. With hundreds, if not thousands of books being released on a daily and weekly basis, it is extremely easy for your book to fall into the background if you are not careful. Effective marketing strategies like the ones you will learn at the end of this book will truly make all of the difference when it comes to making your book a success.

In Conclusion

The difference between book publishing in the past and book publishing now is enormous. The entire face of the industry has evolved as new opportunities have surfaced for virtually every part of the process. When you are in the process of publishing your own book, you will likely find that it is significantly easier than it may have been in the past. However, the ease of the publishing process also means that there are many unique drawbacks that arise now.

The primary drawback is that if you do not have any experience with marketing or you do not learn to market effectively, you likely won't have any success with your book. With so many available, it can be easy for yours to drop into the background and no one to purchase it. Additionally, so many books being released means that every niche is being tapped into on a regular basis and therefore you have to add greater value to your book in order for you to make more sales. Finally, books are selling for much less than ever before. Established and famous authors are still able to sell their books for $10-$30, however those who are not established or well-known will have to sell for significantly lower prices. The average range for e-books is $0.99-$7.99, with the majority being priced around $1.99. That means that each sale will only earn you about $1 worth of profit. Knowing this, you must make many sales in order to see success with your business. Something worth considering, however, is that this lower price point also means that many people will be willing to purchase because the price is so low and therefore it's not a significant investment for them to gain the value from your book. With proper marketing strategies in place, you can earn a healthy residual income as a result.

CHAPTER THREE: GETTING STARTED

Now that you are clear on the evolution of the publishing industry, you are likely wondering how you can get started! As you have learned, there are many factors in your favor when it comes to publishing a book in modern times. If you've ever wanted to write a book, now is the absolute best time for you to get started with it. The process of getting started is without a doubt the most important part of the entire process. You must start strong if you are going to have a powerful book that will rock the online world and earn you a number of sales.

Before You Start

Before you begin with the process of writing a book, you want to make sure that you are completely ready. However, it is important that you don't linger in this step for too long. This is the part where people tend to linger and eventually discourage themselves from writing the book at all. You want to spend just enough time here to cover the following steps and then move on to the next part of the book writing as soon as possible.

The first part is creating a vision for your book. You want to take some time, do some research, and really develop a clear understanding of what you want to write about. To do this, you should start by choosing the field you will be writing in. Generally, you want to choose the field that you are professed in. For example, if you are a financial advisor teaching about finances in your book would be ideal. Once you have decided the general topic, you want to go online and start researching other books that have been written. You will want to complete two sides in this research in order to make sure that you are getting all of the knowledge you need to make your book a success. First, you want to look into the best-selling books for that topic. Second, you want to look into the worst-selling books for that topic. With both, take a note of the following: title, subtitle, cover picture, length of book, specific topic/area of focus, book description, price, reviews, and anything else that may stand out to you.

Once you have done this research, you should have a pretty clear idea as to what the successful sellers have that the unsuccessful ones don't. Then, you want to create a vision that will allow you to remaster the successful sellers as your own work of art. Doing this market research before you get into the details of writing your book will help you significantly in the long run. When you do this, you increase your ability to create a masterpiece that will sell extremely well once it hits the market.

Choosing a Topic

Once you have a vision, you want to choose a specific topic. After your market research, you may have already come up with a topic. If not, take a moment to reconsider which books were the top-sellers. Notice what niche they focused on and if there are any trends between them. If there is, you should consider using this angle as your ideal topic.

In addition to looking for what the best-selling topics are, you should consider what your vision is. Often a non-fiction book is written so that we can share our knowledge and provide greater value to customers that we work with or may potentially work with in the future. It is a chance for you to leverage your business, position yourself as an expert and increase your profits each year. Knowing this, you should be sure to write about something that is going to reflect your business and make sense along the lines of what you are offering clients.

For example, if you are a life coach who specializes in

mindfulness but the best-sellers in life coaching categories are about how to be a life coach, you are not going to want to pay attention to those books. Instead, conduct a little more market research for the topic of mindfulness and see what tends to sell best and what doesn't.

You should never choose a topic just because it is already performing well. Instead, you simply want to make sure it is performing well enough so you aren't writing a book for a market that doesn't exist. Then, you simply want to make sure that you do enough research so that you can produce a high quality book that will definitely sell.

When it comes to making the title for your book, you should always start with a working title. That is, you choose what you think the title and subtitle should be and work with that. Once you complete the book, you can revisit the title and choose one that fits better with what your final product looks like. Choosing a concrete title too early can result in the title not reflecting the book well enough, or the book being restricted to only cover topics that are outlined by the title. The title you start with will almost always be different than the title you end with.

Structuring Your Pages

The next part of the project will actually be writing, but

before you get there you want to understand how your pages should be structured. When you are only writing the rough draft the structure of your pages is not as important. However, having a general structure will ensure that you can still make sense of it all when you return to revise it later on.

The structure is simple. You want to start with your title/subtitle on the first page of your document. Leave the second and third page blank, as these will cover your copyright notice and your table of contents page respectively. Then, on the fourth page you can put in your first chapter. Make sure that the chapter is bolded and large. Throughout the book you will likely add subheadings, so make sure the chapter is large enough to distinguish the difference between that and subheadings.

After you are done with a chapter, always insert a "page break". Simply hitting enter until your text bar is on the next page can result in your pages getting messy when you are going through the editing process. Doing this early can make it a lot easier.

In Microsoft Word, you will notice there is a "design" space. You should use the respective text designs for each part. So, for your title you want to use the "title" setting, for your subtitle use "subtitle", for your chapter titles use "heading 1" and for your subtitles use "heading 2". This will make it easy for everything to be distinguished and understandable.

The Writing Process

Writing your rough draft is extremely easy. You simply have to write. The first time you go through the book there is no need to be too concerned about anything other than getting your thoughts on paper. Of course, you want to group your thoughts together under chapters and subheadings, however that is about the extent of it. Don't worry about spelling, grammar, or anything else. Simply write down all of your thoughts and make sure that you get it all out. Even if two thoughts don't go together well, get them out.

Some people prefer to start by putting bullet points under each chapter and subheading. In doing so, you can outline everything you want to talk about in advance so that you are able to then just type out all of your thoughts afterwards. You may do it in any way that you desire, there is no requirements when it comes to writing out this initial draft. As previously mentioned, the only important part is ensuring that you are getting all of your thoughts out of your mind and onto the document.

After you have gotten the entire document filled with your initial thoughts, you can go back through and rewrite the book. At this point, you still don't need to worry too much about the grammar or spelling. Instead, you simply want to make sure that your sentences, paragraphs and chapters are coherent and flow together well. Later, you can go back through and edit it all.

Understanding Word Count

Many people are unclear on what makes a book "long enough". Word count is highly important as it helps ensure that your book will contain enough information and be valuable enough for your reader. Depending on the topic, you will want to stick close to a certain word-count to ensure that the book is desirable to readers.

For e-books, the average word count is 12,000-15,000 words. This typically puts the document between 30-45 pages, which allows for it to be full of value but not too long for the reading process. For larger books or books that will be printed, you would want to go higher. Between 40,000 and 100,000 or more is typically the suggested word count for a novel. The fewer words, the thinner your book and smaller your pages will be. The more words, the larger the book and the larger the pages as well.

If you are writing with the intention of self-publishing, you are likely writing with the intention of developing an e-book. For that case, make sure that you are between 12,000-15,000 for your final word count. If you want to print your book but also want to have an e-book copy available, try and keep the book between

30,000 and 40,000 words. While many people won't mind reading longer documents on an e-reader, it can become hard on the eyes, therefore causing people to refrain from reading your entire book.

To recall from the beginning of the chapter, the most important part of the entire process is actually starting to write. Whether you take the time to put together the recommended steps from this chapter or not, starting the process of writing is crucial if you are going to write a book. Many people become discouraged because they feel it is too much of a commitment or they simply don't feel like they would be good at it, therefore they don't write a book. The reality is that it is not that difficult to write a high quality book and sell it. Even if you are not particularly good with spelling, grammar, or putting your thoughts into words, you can still write a book. Do the best you can with the writing process, and then hire a good editor to assist you with making the book high quality. There are always ways around the difficulties that you may face when you are getting started.

Ensuring that you take the time to write the book properly from the beginning will save you a significant amount of time in the long run. Instead of having to search for the beginnings and endings of chapters and subsections, you will be able to clearly see where they are. Additionally, you will know how to write a book that will be a success instead of simply writing a book that you hope will be well-received.

Writing a book is not terribly hard. That is why there are hundreds of thousands of people who are publishing books in their lifetime nowadays. Unlike in the past where the process was hard and only those with high talents got through, these days virtually anyone can write a book. While that does mean that the market is full, it also means that you do not need to have an English Major or other special degree or talent to ensure that you can write a book. You simply need a topic, motivation, and a desire to create something that will add value to other people's lives. As a result, you will have a book that will allow you to make sales and add "self-published author" to your tagline on your resume. It really is a win-win situation!

CHAPTER FOUR: STAYING MOTIVATED

Many people have had writer's block in their writing career. If you think back to the last chapter, we discussed how some people never even begin writing their books. In a sense, this is like a type of writer's block. In fact, it is the most lethal kind. Once you actually convince yourself to start writing your book, none of the writer's block or fading motivation will compare to the courage it took to actually start writing.

Still, writer's block and lack of motivation can crawl up and make the process of actually finishing your book project difficult. That is why you should know exactly how you need to respond to these situations to keep yourself steadily moving towards the goal: a finished book. The following tips and steps will assist you with curbing your writer's block and reclaiming your motivation to ensure that your book becomes a completed project.

Working Through Writer's Block

Many writers tend to experience writer's block at one point or another during the process of writing their books. Some may even experience writer's block several times throughout the process. Writer's block is completely normal, even the most experienced writers will experience it regularly. The important thing to remember is that it's not the writer's block itself but rather what you do about it that counts. If you experience writer's block, it's imperative that you do not walk away from your book and allow that to stop you from writing anything further. Instead, you need to work through the writer's block.

Writer's block can be difficult to curb, especially if you don't know what you're doing. Many people are unaware that it can easily be subsided with a few simple steps so that they can resume the writing process and complete their master piece. In order to curb your own writer's block, work through the following steps:

1. Stop writing the book for a while. Occasionally, writing for one single subject can become difficult and can result in people not writing as well. Try using words and writing to practice a different art form so that you can release any blocks and start writing freely again. A great art you can do for this

process is taking a piece of blank paper and using words to create a picture. You may use several written words to create the outline for something such as a flower, or you may write the words through the center and use it as though it is a colorful filler. Whatever you choose to do, make it personal and continue doing it until you feel you are writing freely.

2. If you notice you are getting writer's block during the writing process, stop writing immediately. Trying to push through it can result in you feeling stressed because the pressure makes the writer's block get worse and worse. Instead, take a break from your writing completely. Turn off your computer, walk away and do everything you can to take your mind off of your writing. The less you think about it, the better. That way, when you return to it later you will be feeling refreshed and ready to carry on with your book.

3. Sometimes a change of scenery is a great way to get yourself refreshed. Keep a notepad handy just in case you get inspired, but don't rely on the change of pace to inspire you. Instead, allow it to release everything from your mind and refresh you once again. A great change of scenery is to go for a walk somewhere outside of your neighborhood. Nature trails, walking around a local lake or creek, and other nature walks are a wonderful place to head to if you are feeling tied down by writer's block.

4. Read someone else's work. Although you do not want to copy their work, reading someone else's

book on a similar subject can help re-inspire you to stay on track and continue writing. Sometimes writer's block is a result of us not having enough inspiration for what we are working on. When you read someone else's completed project you will gain new insight on what you are attempting to create and therefore you will get an idea of how you can move forward with your project.

5. Read what you've already written. Don't reread the last sentence or paragraph over and over. Instead, read the entire project from the beginning to where you are stuck. Sometimes writers have a tendency to get writer's block because they cannot picture the flow in their mind, therefore they don't know how to keep going. Reading over your own work can remind you what flow you are working with and can help you keep the flow going so that your book comes out nicely and you can work past the block.

Writer's block can be extremely stressful to deal with, especially if you don't know how. Many people believe that writer's block is a failure or a sign that they are not competent enough to write the project they have set out to write. The reality is that it actually happens to many people. Often, it is simply from lack of inspiration or losing your train of thought when you are writing. Regardless of how many times it happens, you must always work through it and keep going. Once you have the rough draft completed, you have finished the hardest part. Give yourself the opportunity to finish this piece and you will be well on your way to having a completed book that you can publish and sell to your clients.

Staying Motivated

Aside from writer's block, many people struggle with staying motivated. This differs from writer's block because there is nothing that is mentally stopping you from moving forward with the writing. In other words, you likely know exactly what you want to write next. However, writing it can be stressful. For people who don't write on a regular basis or who have never written something as long as a book before, actually completing it can be hard. Books are a lot longer and take more focus and effort that people generally think they do. Because of that, it can become easy to feel like it is "too long" and lose motivation to stay committed to the process.

When you are writing your own book, you certainly don't want a lack of motivation to come between you and your success. Setting out to write a book is a commitment, and it can be a difficult commitment at that. Sometimes you will wonder why you ever started. Sometimes you will want to know what made you think it was a good idea. You might even question if you are the right person for the job, or if you actually know what you are doing well enough to actually be doing it. If you aren't careful, you might feel overwhelmed by the number of published books in your field, maybe even to the point that you start comparing your abilities to theirs. The reality is, if you are writing about a subject that you are passionate about and you are going to be able to write a high quality book regardless of your writing experience.

Many people forget to realize that when you are writing a book, the first draft is only a rough draft. You still have the opportunity to go back through the book and ensure that everything flows the way you want it to. Then, you can send it to a proofreader and an editor. The extra assistance will ensure that you are left with a book that is high quality and that no one realizes you have no experience with writing.

If you are seriously concerned about your writing abilities, there are other options you can go. For example, many people use ghostwriters or co-authors to complete their books. Ghostwriters write a book and you take the credit, and co-authors are listed as a part of the author section but if you get the right contract then the co-author would be the one doing all the writing. All you have to do, then, is provide your information and ideas for what you want added into the book.

Still, it is not necessary for you to hire help if you don't want to. If you truly want a book that you wrote on the market, you can certainly do so. Maintaining motivation can be difficult, but there are many ways that you can. The following tips will help you recharge your motivation if you need to:

1. Have a writing schedule. When you specifically schedule times into your calendar when you are going to write, it can be harder to skip over it. Discipline yourself so that whenever "writing" comes up on your calendar, you sit down and write at least a few words at a time.

2. Remove the pressure. There is no need to write an entire half of your book in a single sitting. If you have several ideas coming through, write them down in a notepad before you start writing, or as you are writing. Then, stay focused on the single area that you are writing in that moment. Take your time. Don't feel as though you need to write a whole bunch each time you sit down. If you only write 500 words one day but you write 5000 the next, it is absolutely nothing to be concerned of. The primary focus is to ensure that you are sitting down and writing on a consistent basis.

3. Consider having a working deadline. Some people will start marketing their book before they've even started it and that can add pressure to the project. If you're the kind of person who experiences pressure this way, consider having a working deadline that can be adjusted based on how quickly you are writing the book. This is also a great idea for people who have never written a longer project before. If you are new to writing longer projects, you may not have any idea how long it takes you to write such things. While the internet can give you a guess, your own process is going to be different

from other people's. At least with your first project, give yourself a break and relieve the pressure of overly marketing the book before you're absolutely sure about when it will be done. Pick your final deadline when you are in the last ¼ of the book, that way you have a strong idea as to how quickly you are finishing and how much the rest of it will take. Always budget in time for editors, formatters, and the actual publishing process when you are setting your overall project deadline.

4. Have a fixed deadline. If you don't work well with an unfixed finishing line, or if you are unclear on how long it takes you to write longer projects, consider having a fixed deadline. For some people, knowing that the deadline is coming encourages them to write more. It can make them feel a jolt of "I need to get this done" instead of "I have plenty of time life" which can make all the difference when it comes to actually writing a book.

5. Recruit an accountability partner. Sometimes having someone who regularly asks you how you are doing is beneficial when it comes to staying accountable for your goal and actually completing it. When you are writing a book, having an accountability partner can be extremely helpful. The partner doesn't necessarily need to be writing their own book. Instead, it just needs to be someone who is willing to make sure that you are staying on track with your goal and that you are working towards the finishing line. They should also be someone who can give you words of encouragement if you are struggling, need

inspiration, or need motivation. Accountability partners can significantly improve the rate at which you finish your book.

Staying motivated can be difficult, especially with a project that is large. While some people have no issue staying motivated, others can become overwhelmed or even bored part way through the project. It is not uncommon to have this happen, especially considering the length that book projects tend to be. There are many ways that you can combat a lack of motivation to make sure that you actually finish your project and are able to market it to the public and make sales. The primary key is to make sure that you recognize when you are becoming unmotivated and quickly work to resolve the issue by finding a way to get motivated. The longer you are unmotivated and refrain from writing your book, the less likely it will be that you return to the project to complete it.

Hitting Word Count

When you are writing a book, especially if you have never written one before, hitting word count can be pretty difficult. Although it may not seem like a large amount when you are reading it, 12,000-15,000 words or more can be a lot when you are the one writing the book. You may find that you fall short of the word count and struggle to actually hit it. Alternatively, you may find that you have many more words than your ideal word count and that your edging on having a book that will be too long. Regardless of what your issue is, there is always a way to resolve it.

When You Aren't Hitting Word Count

If you're struggling to hit your word count, there are a few things that you can do to resolve this and ensure that you end up with a book that is long enough while still providing value. The most important thing is to make sure that you do not fluff up the book. Writing sentences in a long-winded format and adding unnecessary words can lead to having a book that is all filler and that lacks value. You want to make sure that the book you are offering has a high value for those who invest in it so that they want to invest in more that you have to offer them.

The first step you can take towards getting your book up to word count is reviewing each chapter. Notice anywhere that could have been explained better, or anything that may be missing. Ultimately, you want to see where you can add more value to your book so that the reader gains even more knowledge from reading it. Highlight these places so that you can go back and write more in this area. Once you have highlighted all of them, go ahead and write more into these sections so that you are able to get closer to your word count.

Next, consider the way your information is laid out. Did

you condense certain things that could have been their own unique headings or subjects? If so, break these down and write more on these subjects. Elaborate enough that readers will gain a high level of information from each section or chapter and that they are thoroughly informed about the subject by the time they are done reading.

If you have added more value to your book but are still struggling to reach word count, consider reviewing the subject of your book. Is it too narrow? Or is it something that there simply isn't enough information around for you to provide greater knowledge? If either of these are the case, consider picking a slightly broader topic that will allow you to go into greater depth so that you can add even more information to your book.

In some cases, you may find that you have picked a topic that simply doesn't warrant an entire book. If this is the case and you can't broaden it in a logical method, you may want to consider writing a different book. For the one you have already been writing, if you have enough words (over 5,000) you might consider turning it into a smaller e-book-only project. That way you can still release a book while you go back through the process of writing about a broader subject that will allow you to hit a greater word count.

If you are only falling short of your word count by about 1000 words or less, you should not worry to greatly. Word counts are generally averages, and they vary greatly depending on the subject and the format of your book. Small discrepancies like this are not enough to make or break your book's success, therefore you don't need to consider them. Often times the editing process will find areas where slightly more can be added to bring you closer to your word count.

When You're Way Over Word Count

Word counts are usually on a spectrum and the spectrum is generally very broad. If you are in the top sector of the spectrum for your desired project, that is no problem. However, if you are going way over (more than 1000-2000 words over) you will be going too far over and your book will become too long. If a book is too long, many people won't read it. People enjoy books that are just long enough to provide them with all of the information that they need to know. Nothing more, nothing less.

You should adjust your word count so that it is a more appropriate length. How you do this will depend on what has caused you to have such a high word count. If your word count is high because you are going into too great of detail on subjects that people don't actually need to know about or are irrelevant to your book, you need to adjust that. Make sure you go back through your pages and that you eliminate any unnecessary information or filler that may be taking up word space in your book.

If your numbers are going over because you have so much information to share, you need to consider the topic you've chosen. If you are going way over word count, you have likely chosen a topic that is too broad. In this case, you may want to choose a narrower topic that will prevent you from going over. Alternatively, you may want to turn your topic into a "series topic" and choose sub-topics underneath it. Each sub-topic can then be put into its own book. For example, you may have a mini-series on renovating houses. Book one may be about bathrooms and kitchens, book two about living rooms and bedrooms, and book three may be about the exterior of your house. This way, you have managed to talk about your chosen topic but you have turned it into a higher value project that still meets the criteria for your word count.

Going over the total numbers in word count is not a big deal. It simply means that you are highly knowledgeable in your field and that you need to adjust how you are writing the project. Simply adjust your goal so that each book is a manageable and valuable piece and you will have a successful series of books on your hands in no time!

CHAPTER FIVE: FINISHING YOUR BOOK

Once you have finished your rough draft, you are ready to move into the final stages of finishing your book. The rough draft is the hardest and longest part of the entire process of writing a book. After that, it's extremely simple.

Proofreaders and Editors

The first thing you are going to want to do is send your book off to a proofreader and editor. This is someone who will read through the book to ensure that the information is displayed well and that it can be read easily. The editor will make sure that the grammar is accurate and you have spelled everything correctly. Any adjustments will be made at this time. They may send your project back for you to make the adjustments, or they may do so for you. Then, you will have an edited book that is almost ready to go!

There are many places to find editors if you don't already have one. Many websites such as peopleperhour.com have a series of editors available for hire who can help you with this process for an extremely reasonable rate. You simply have to go in, pick someone who can do your job effectively, and then give them the work. They will do all of the rest for you and then send it back to you as a completed project.

The price you pay for an editor will vary. It depends on who you hire and what experience they have, typically. It can also depend on where you hire them from. You should be prepared to spend a bit of money on this process, however, as everyone will charge some level of money. The only way you may get this process completed for free is if you are friends with an editor.

Formatting the Manuscript

When the editor is done with your project, they are going send it back to you with all of the edits completed. Then, you will have to format your manuscript. This means that you will do the final layout for how the book will be read by future readers. You want to include your title page, your copyright page, your clickable table of contents, and each chapter. You may also want to include a disclaimer, depending on who the book is being written for. Now is also the time that you would want to add any pictures and choose your fonts for the project. The most common fonts are Arial, Times New Roman, and Palatino Linotype. These fonts are the easiest to read for a long period of time.

Make sure that you spend some time really laying out your book. You want it to be laid out in a way that is attractive and readable. Consider your book your masterpiece, and this is the part where you really get to bring it all together. Now you have the written word part of the art piece completed and it is time to put together the aesthetic part of the art piece. While you don't need to spend several hours here, spending a few hours really putting it together nicely will help make sure that your readers have a highly enjoyable experience and are happily willing to recommend your book to others.

Final Proofread

The final part of the entire process with your book itself is the last proofread. Ideally you want to do this part yourself but also have one or two others proof read it with you. Having a few sets of eyes looking over your project will ensure that nothing goes unnoticed. That way, you can have a polished off project to sell to your future readers. Make sure that if you get other people proofreading your project now that they are meticulous and are willing to openly let you know what changes they think would add value to your book. It greatly helps when one or more of these individuals are experienced with the book writing and formatting process.

Publishing

The last step is to publish! Using your chosen platform, go ahead and get your book published! For a program like Amazon, all you have to do is go through the steps that Amazon will walk you through. If it is your first time, you may have to create a publisher profile so that you can claim the rights to your book.

Most times the publishing process will require that you have a short description about the book itself. Give yourself some time to make a description that is catchy and informative and truly encourages people to want to read more. Don't give away any intricate details of your book, but be sure to give potential buyers a clear idea of what they will learn from your book.

Having a book that has been completed and put live for sales is an exciting process. You officially have become a published author at this point. Or, a multiple-times published author if this isn't your first time. You should take some time to congratulate yourself for making it this far. Many people struggle to finish writing a book and actually publish it because the process can be long and sometimes difficult. If you've made it this far, you can already consider yourself a success!

CHAPTER SIX: MARKETING YOUR BOOK

Getting your book completed and publishing it is exciting, but if you're not making any sales then your book likely isn't completing the task that you wanted it to. While you may have many motives for writing a book, it is almost certain that earning a residual income is one of those motives. In order to start making some sales on your book, you are going to want to market it! The following ideas are several proven ways that you can market your book, varying in expenses so that you can market it no matter what your budget is.

Build Up the Hype

During the writing process, you should spend some time building the hype. If you were working with a working deadline, start building the hype without promising a finished date. Then, once you do have an ideal published date, you can start building the hype around that, too. You can do so by posting about your book regularly. Let people know how it felt to write the book, why they should be excited for the release, and what type of value they can expect to gain from it. Don't give away too many intimate details of the book, but share enough that people gain curiosity and want to read it when it is released. You may even publish one or two quotes from the book and explain how much further into detail it will go so that people get a clear idea of exactly what they can expect when they read your book.

Word of Mouth

Once your book has been published, word of mouth is huge. Getting people to actually review your book after they have read it is important. It is also important to ask them that they share the title with their friends who may be interested as well. The more people who read it, the more people who will rave about it. That means more people will want to read it and therefore it will be purchased more. Although there are many marketing methods out there, this continues to be one of the best ones so far. Many people rely on social proof before they purchase something. If you have positive social proof in your favor, then you are much more likely to continue making book sales.

Paid Advertisements

Although they do cost some money, posting paid advertisements can increase the amount of visibility your book receives. Paid advertisements can be posted through Amazon, as well as through a number of different social media platforms. These advertisements can be extremely successful at getting your product in front of viewers who would be most likely to purchase it. That way, you increase your visibility as well as interest in your book.

Influencers

Many companies use influencers to sell their projects and it is a highly valuable format. Influencers can help increase your audience for very cheap, often even free. Giving a free copy of your book to relevant influencers in your industry means that they will review it in front of their audience thus giving you a free "in" to their audience. Since they have already built rapport and trust with this audience, you know that these people will be much more likely to purchase your book. Ideally, you want to give your product to 2-4 major influencers in your market or 4-6 smaller ones. That way you can get in front of several audiences. Plus, the more influencers that are talking about your book, the better!

Listed in Multiple Places

Listing your book on multiple platforms can greatly increase your visibility. While Amazon.com is the most popular, there are many other indie platforms that people look to when they are in the process of purchasing a new book. Posting on multiple platforms not only gets you a greater audience but it also gets you into a position where people will see your book title several times over. As a result, they will think it is highly important and that they must read it!

Exclusive Sales

Having exclusive sales when you are launching your book is another great way to have a successful launch date. Selling copies for a discounted rate for your launch means that you can increase the amount of sales you make. Sales give people more inclination towards purchasing because sales are generally only short-term *and* they equate to even more savings for the buyer. The get a "why not?" outlook which means that they will be more likely to purchase your product. Doing this on launch date means that you get the initial sales out of the way. After that, social proof and word of mouth should help carry you!

Ask Book Stores to Carry It

Many people don't realize that you can actually ask book stores to carry your book. If you have a printed copy and you have a proper ISBN number, most book stores will carry your book for you. Simply reach out to their customer service department and request for them to carry your book! While some places may say no, you'd likely be surprised to how many will carry it for you.

Market it On Your Website

If you have a website that you already use for your business and your book is relevant to your business (or at least slightly relevant) posting it on your website is a great idea. This means that you will be viewed as even more of an expert in your field, and that you are getting more publicity for your book. Anyone who wanders to your website to learn about your services and offerings will learn about your book, and may be even more inclined to purchase it. If you want to take it a step further, considering offering them an exclusive discount in exchange for them signing up for your e-mail newsletter. That way they can get the book for a cheaper price and you can also have their e-mail so you can send them information about other services you have available as well.

There are many ways to market your book. It is important that you stay consistent with the marketing process. You want your book to continue having a successful selling period for as long as possible. While books still have a life span and yours will eventually stop making as many sales, it is important that you do your part to keep that life span as long as possible.

The ways described in this chapter are the best methods for marketing your book in an inexpensive manner that can be done by anyone. You can market your book in other ways, too, however. Book sales, trade markets, and consignment shops are all great areas to market your book. You can also have friends post it on their websites and talk about your book, complete interviews on famous podcasts, and do as much possible to encourage people to talk about your book on a regular basis. The ultimate goal is to get it into the eye of the public and keep it there as long as you can.

CONCLUSION

Writing a book is an exceedingly popular way to market your business and position yourself as an expert in your industry. While there are already many books on the market, there is always room for yours as well. If you want to write a book, there is virtually nothing stopping you from doing so.

In the past, people had to rely on publishing chains and booksellers to get their books in front of the public and make sales. If they couldn't get through publishing chains, they couldn't get into bookstores unless they had an enormous amount of money to print the books themselves. It was almost unheard of to hear of writers getting their books published without the assistance of a proper publishing chain.

The past thirty years has brought an enormous revolution to the book publishing industry. Anyone can publish a book now, so long as they have access to a computer and some editing software. Of course, there are still certain things you want to emphasize on if you are going to write a book that will be high quality and valuable to your readers. *How to Write a Book: A Blueprint for How To Write, Publish And Market Your Very Own Non-fiction Book* is fully intended to be a guidebook to help you write your very own book and sell it on the market.

I hope this book was able to provide you with a highly valuable blueprint that successfully walked you through the process of writing your own book. By now you should be clear on how to pick a quality topic, write your book, edit and format it, and get it published. You should also have a good idea as to how you can market your book so that you can earn a profit from your work.

The next step is for you to start writing if you haven't already. If you have not been writing as you read this book, then I encourage you to go back to chapter 3 and get started. Find a topic you want to write about, do some research, and then get to writing! The sooner you start writing, the sooner you will be done writing your very own book. Then, you can move on to publishing it and calling yourself a published author!

Finally, if you enjoyed this book and felt it guided you through the process of writing your own book well, I ask that you please take the time to write an honest review on Amazon Kindle. Your feedback would be greatly appreciated as I'm a self-publisher just like you.

Thank you and wishing you great success!

www.ingramcontent.com/pod-product-compliance
Lightning Source LLC
Chambersburg PA
CBHW071119280526
45787CB00003B/1094